This is a true story based on my life experiences.

I have changed the names of some characters and for others, don't mention their names at all in order to protect their privacy.

No part of this book may be reproduced, or stored in a retrieval system, or transmitted in any form or by any means, electronic, mechanical, photocopying, recording, or otherwise, without the express written permission of the publisher.

ISBN   978-1-300-60491-4

Among the Twinkling Stars

Story and Art by Charis Alfonso

To those who have always been there for me and my family, thank you.

My Parents, My Angels

Some people walk through life quietly, leaving only footprints. My parents, however, left behind a legacy of love, kindness, and strength that will never fade.

My mom was more than just my mother — she was a protector, a friend to all, and, too many, a guardian angel. She had a way of making friends wherever she went, warmth that drew people in. She loved deeply, stood up for her family, and even saved lives.

I remember at a Downey High School track meet, there was a boy who was so dehydrated that he collapsed in the stands. My mom didn't hesitate — she ran to him, gave him what he needed to rehydrate, and helped him recover. And one night, my mom and I saw a truck flip over at a gas station, she told me to stay put and rushed to save the driver, pulling him out and keeping him conscious until help arrived. She was fearless. She was strong.

She fought hard when she was diagnosed with breast cancer, but the disease took her from us too soon. I was at school when I found out. A teacher pulled me out of class and took me downstairs to meet my little brother, Jeremiah.

He told me she was gone.

The night before, my mom had reassured me with her usual strength, saying, "Hey baby, don't you worry. I'll be there when you break that record. I'll be cheering. Okay, baby?" I wanted so badly to believe her. So, I did. I believed that she would be there and that everything would be okay.

Losing her shattered me, and it changed all of us. I remember my brother Jonathan sobbing at her funeral, unable to stop. He was never the same. None of us were.

Then, I lost my dad.

My dad was a gentle soul—quiet, but filled with warmth. Everyone who knew him described him as a big teddy bear. I remember a birthday party he planned for me and my little brother, Jeremiah. Our birthdays were pretty close together. His on

May 27th and mine June 2nd. A few of our good friends showed up, my dad wanted it to be special. I caught him crying that day. When I asked if he was okay, he simply said, "Your mom would have loved this."

One evening, I found my dad looking through my sketchbook. He smiled and said, "Charis, these are really great. Do me a favor, okay? Never stop drawing. You're gonna be somebody someday, so keep at it. Your mother was always so proud of you."

I nodded, "I promise."

Not long after, he started feeling unwell. It got worse, and I called an ambulance. My oldest brother Charles went with him, and when he came home, he reassured me that our dad just needed rest. But that night, we got the call. A nurse told Charles to get to the hospital. A part of me knew that something was wrong but I kept telling myself, "No, dad will be okay. My dad is okay. Everything is okay. We will be okay."

A doctor tried to soften the blow, but nothing could have prepared me. My dad was gone. Heart failure, they said. But I believe he died of a broken heart.

I held his hand one last time. It was ice cold. The warmth was gone. Just two months after my mom left us, my dad was gone too.

I remember thinking, "I need to call Michael, and I need to let my other brothers know that dad's gone. I asked a nurse if I could use the phone and called home. My brother Michael answered the phone and I told him, "Dad's gone. He's gone."

The Vultures

My world was spiraling out of control and things were happening way too fast. I wanted it all to stop. Our friends came to my family's side, trying to help us during this difficult time. They were our family, doing their best to help us figure out what came next.

Then came the people who claimed to be friends with my parents, vultures in disguise, the Graves family. My older brothers Charles and Michael were friends with their cousin but my parents never mentioned being close with them.

It was the day of my father's funeral at a church we had only been to once before but since the pastor offered to help; my oldest brother Charles accepted their offer. Little did we know, the only reason they were being so nice is because they wanted the donation money that was being gifted to my brothers and I by our friends and people who saw our story on the news. The pastor of this church and the Graves convinced my brother Charles to have the money sent to the church to hold for us. We were still broken by everything that had happened that we agreed because we thought that they were just being nice.

The service was nice and a lot of our friends were there. Before my father's funeral started, one of my older brothers, Jonathan arrived. He was the second oldest. I saw him enter the front door and I went over to give him a hug but the pastor's daughter, immediately came over and told him that he wasn't allowed inside. I didn't understand.

It was our dad's funeral. Then, Mrs. Graves showed up and said, "He's drunk, don't let him in." But, he wasn't drunk. He was sad and had clearly been crying but they didn't want to let him inside. My brother didn't want to cause any trouble even though he hadn't done anything wrong. He told me that it was okay and that he would talk to me and our other brothers later. I promised him that I would tell them that he did come by. He smiled and gave me a hug.

I was angry but was told that it was fine and that my brother shouldn't be there. It wasn't right. I knew that but back then, it was hard for me to speak up when something was bothering me, hard for me to say no. I didn't want to make anyone mad at me. Looking back, I wish I was stronger and would have yelled at them. My brother did belong there. Later, I found out that my dad's best friend tried to get in to the funeral as well but like my brother, was not allowed inside.

After the funeral our friends and even my mother's brother Kevin asked us if we would like to spend the night so we could talk about how they might be able to help us and just to have a place to stay for the moment. I said, "That sounds good." But, I remember my brothers telling me that the Graves family had offered us to spend the night. The mother said, "It's just for tonight. We have a big house with a lot of rooms, so you can all sleep comfortably." My brothers had already agreed to spend the night and I wanted to be where they were, so I agreed to go. That night, the youngest son, Adder, took me to the garage and said that I would be sleeping there. He said that he made me a bed and that it would be comfortable. I couldn't stop thinking how his mother, Morrisa said that we would all be sleeping in rooms. She never mentioned one of us having to sleep in the garage. I thanked Adder and sat down on the bed. He sat next to me and said, "I'm here if you need anything, okay?" His smile seemed genuine but for some reason his eyes looked dead. Like he didn't mean what he was saying. I nodded and went to sleep after he left.

The next morning I was woken up by Adder. He had a twin sister named Sierra who was bigger than he was, taller and bulky. She seemed nice. Adder had a more delicate appearance.

"You will stay, right?" He asked me as I was barely opening my eyes.

"Huh?" I said confused. Why would I be staying? We were only supposed to spend the night.

It had seemed that when I was asleep, the Graves family had already convinced my brothers to stay. I didn't say much. I just said, "Okay." I had already lost so much and only wanted to be where my brothers were. Four of my brothers were there with me. Jonathan was staying with a friend. I called him letting him know where we were. He was surprised but asked if everyone was okay. I told him that we were fine. Jonathan sounded uncertain if I was really fine or just saying that I was. He told me to keep him updated with everything.

When Jonathan did come by, he was immediately told that he was not allowed to see us, that if he cared he would have taken us in. What? That didn't make sense but it was something they would echo to all our friends who tried to contact us. My uncle Kevin even came by and wanted to see if we were okay. At this point, the Vultures had dug their claws in deep making us afraid to speak up. It was like our tongues had been cut off, unable to speak the truth.

They took us in with warm smiles and empty promises, swearing they were family friends, that they only wanted to help. But it was all a lie. They wanted the donation money.

That's all we ever were to them—a way to profit.

They isolated us, cutting us off from our friends. If we wanted to talk to them, we could only do so at school, but even then, it was hard for us tell our friends what was really going on. Every day, we were verbally abused, insulted, and pushed aside once they had gotten what they wanted. And when that wasn't enough, the cruelty escalated.

Every day in that house was a nightmare. We were blamed for things we did not do. There was a time after the Graves got their house remodeled and I was home alone with Adder. I will never forget that day. It's forever ingrained in my mind. We were told to clean the entire house. Adder was a clean freak and if I didn't do things like he wanted, he would tell me, "Hey, let's take a break. Come in my room." I hesitated but followed him. He towered over me as I looked up at him.

He smirked and said, "You're weak. How will you ever defend yourself? I'll teach you to fight back." I didn't understand. This was coming out of nowhere. I laughed at the ridiculousness, "What do you mean? I don't want to 'train' with you. We should get back to cleaning before your mom gets mad at us."

I don't know if that's what set him off or if he was already mad about something else that day but he swung at me nearly punching me in the face. I didn't know what to do.

He kept saying over and over, "You're weak! Fight back!"

I replied, "I can't." My voice was barely above a whisper.

He then tripped me and held me on the floor as he pressed himself against me whispering in my ear, "See how easy this is? Imagine if it's someone else. What will you do then? I want to help you. Won't you let me help? Now, try to get me off of you."

I tried, but it was no use. He may have looked delicate but he was so strong. I couldn't do anything. My tiny wrists felt like they were twigs as he held them down. Eventually, he grew bored and let me go but that wasn't the last time he would do something like that. He never went further than that but he always made me feel like he was going to. Being able to pin down someone like me is something I think he enjoyed. Adder always got what he wanted.

How could he tell me that he was my friend and treat me like that? How could he steal my first kiss and turn around, pin me down making me feel like he would break me further. What the fuck was with these mind games?! I only saw him as a friend because when we first moved in, he was nice. I wasn't looking for anything else but he kept moving in wanting me locked at his side and when his family had something to say, he wouldn't defend me. He would stand there smirking as his parents accused me of being weird and obsessed. I wasn't doing anything. I wanted to be left alone.

I sometimes wondered why he chose me to pick on. I thought about how he said things happened in his past that shaped who he was back then, but could he really use that as an excuse to always corner me when no one else was around? He knew I wouldn't say, "No" I wouldn't speak up. I was too weak; a vase that could shatter if pushed too far off the ledge.

He wanted to teach me to be stronger but in his own cruel way. His hands squeezing my wrists hurt. The weight of him on me was suffocating but as always, there was something wrong with me. I wasn't strong, couldn't fight back, a broken doll unable to be fixed.

The manipulation of Adder was just has poisonous as his mother. He was the mama's boy who could do no wrong.

It was him, not me but it was always me in their eyes. Their blindness to their son's bullshit was astonishing. I hated him but at the same time, he made me feel sorry for him. Remember his childhood was hard. He would do something and it was like I couldn't say anything because he went through something.

I wanted to scream, "What about what you're doing now?! It's not okay!"

Just because you've been hurt, doesn't give you the right to hurt others. My mother would always say, "Two wrongs don't make a right." Why was this so hard for people to understand?

But, I tried to ignore the pain.

Endure.

Mute

The father of the Graves, Anwir was a drunk, and creepy. The kind of man who made my skin crawl. After they got their house remodeled, I had my own room. I would draw to try and escape everything around me, still there was no privacy. Mrs. Graves would make fun of me for always being in my room drawing and Mr. Graves would at times come in my room at night and just stare at me. I don't know for how long but I pretended to be asleep every time. I wondered if his wife even cared. I doubt it. I think it was hilarious to her, "Oh look at Anwir, such a funny guy."

I came back one day from school and saw that Mr. Graves was drinking a beer and watching someone he hired to break up the pavement in front of their house. The people from the show who remodeled their house put my family's last name Higgins above the Graves family name. Anwir didn't like that. So, he had some guy smash it to pieces even though he said before that we were all family. He told the people who rebuilt his house that he loved what they had written because it meant a lot to him since he loved our parents. I guess that was all for the cameras. He never loved them. He would constantly insult them saying how our parents didn't teach my brothers and me anything because we lacked 'common sense'. He said that a lot when he was trying to make a point, always trying to put us down.

I tried to go inside the house but Mr. Graves made me stand there and watch as the concrete was smashed into over and over again. He saw how upset I was but he just smiled and took more sips of his beer.

It had gotten so bad and I wanted to tell my friends but I was afraid of that family and what they might do. Mr. Graves was very intimidating and made me feel like if I told anyone what was happening, something bad might happen.

Before the Graves got their house remodeled, they had a house party and only invited their family and friends. Our friends weren't invited because they repeated over and over that our friends didn't care about us. They said my brothers and I had to attend the party. I didn't want to. I didn't like anyone there and their cousins would always bully me calling me a "mute" Anwir would just laugh and say that the only word I knew was, "Hi." I was constantly treated like I was stupid. Told my hair looked dirty when I had just washed it or just gotten it done at the salon by this nice lady named Peggy who offered to do my braids for free. She asked me every time I went to go see her if I was okay and if the Graves were mistreating me, but I couldn't speak up. I told her everything was fine when it wasn't.

At that party, I didn't speak because I didn't want to talk to people who treated me like shit. They still forced me to be involved somehow. I was only there for them to mock and they always made sure to do it when my brothers weren't around. They knew I wouldn't say anything. That I would just continue to pretend like everything was fine. Their cousins called me, "Ugly" and other things I don't want to repeat. Mr. and Mrs. Graves did nothing but laugh along with them.

I've been called ugly before so, I guess I started to believe it. I was always a target for someone to make fun of. My mom would always reassure me that I was beautiful no matter what anyone said. She was always there standing up for me when bullies would harass me or try to beat me up but she couldn't help me at this house with these vultures. I wished she was there. I wished my dad was there to say something but I couldn't call them to help. I just let people beat me up emotionally like it was just another day, "This is normal. It's supposed to happen."

I hated that day with their stupid party celebrating what? How amazing they thought they were.

I was sitting down and the oldest son, Birsha came and picked me up. He tried to throw me in the pool even though at the time he knew that I couldn't swim. I kicked and screamed but he didn't put me down until my brothers saw what was happening and stepped in.

Of course, their mother saw all this and thought it was so hilarious.

Birsha thought he could do what he wanted and get away with it because his parents allowed his behavior and always bailed him out when he got in trouble. He was so tough though, wasn't he?

Pathetic.

My family had been through so much during the time we were there that it had felt like we were there for years. All we wanted was for them to care like they said they did the day they asked us to stay.

The Graves had cruel intentions from the start, from Birsha and his father picking my brother Josh up, throwing him in a chair and cutting his hair when he wanted to grow out his hair so he could braid it, telling my brother Jeremiah that he smelled on a daily basis, the constant harassment of my brother Charles. Making him feel like a failure when all he has ever done was step up when our dad passed away and did his best to make sure we were all okay.

Jeremiah and Josh would have football games and the Graves would purposely sit on the other side of the stands across from us and cheer for the other team. The Graves seemed to hate Downey for some reason. They knew how my mom loved the city and she adored Downey High School yet, they continued their taunting saying, "I hope you lose today." They never cheered for us to do good, only ever wanting to see us fail so they could rub it in our faces.

Soon, after they got all that they wanted, they pushed us all to the side. Morrisa and Anwir made up a dumb reason to kick Michael and Charles out. They were mad that they went to the movies with their friends but their son Birsha also tagged along with his girlfriend. My brothers and their son told them ahead of time and they said they were okay with it. Arriving back before 9pm like they asked them to but they still told them to leave. It was out of nowhere.

You see, they invited friends from Downey. They were real childhood friends that our parents knew and trusted.

They couldn't stand it.

At the time I was upset but it was a blessing that they didn't have to deal with their insults anymore. Charles tried to grab some of their things and our parents' pictures but the Graves only allowed them to take what they said was okay to leave with. The gaming console my dad had gifted to my brothers and I was left in that house because

Birsha said that it was actually theirs and didn't belong to us.

Not too long after this, I had a track meet that I needed to go to. I knew the Graves wouldn't let me go but I needed to run. I promised my mother that I would keep running and compete until my team was fast enough to beat the school record in the 4x400 meter relay. I picked up the phone and called my Godmother Sharon. I told her that I had a track meet and didn't want to be late. She said, "I got you baby. On my way."

As soon as I got off the phone and headed downstairs, Birsha and his mother were standing by the front door. They told me that I couldn't leave. My eyes widened, "You were listening?"

They didn't say anything. I gathered the strength and pushed passed them. I knew they would have something to say when I got back but they knew how important it was for me to keep running. The people, who swore to have loved our parents, didn't even show up to my mother's funeral. Only coming around after my dad passed away and they heard about the donation money and knew they would get their home remodeled if we were there.

Vultures.

It took everything in me, but I finally gathered the courage to leave one morning. I was getting my things from my desk and dresser when Birsha came in my room saying, "You're not allowed to do that. Those things don't belong to you."

I told him that they were my things; I was going to go back get my diary that my dad had given me but I was being blocked. He grabbed my track bag and demanded that I open it.

As if something had awakened inside of me, I yelled, "Let go!" He stopped fighting with me but still blocked my way so I couldn't go back in my room for my diary.

Looking up at mom and dad's pictures hanging on the wall, I tried to take them down but Birsha placed his hand on the frames and said, "No. These stay here."

"Let me take them. It's my parents." I replied almost in tears.

"They're not here are they?" Birsha said coldly staring down at me. There was nothing I could do at the time. I left thinking that I would be able to get my diary and my parents pictures somehow later on but I didn't realize that I would never see my diary again and they would try to use it against my family and me later.

My two younger brothers Jeremiah and Josh followed soon after me. At track practice that same day, I had told my friend Marie and Josh that I wasn't going back and how our parent's pictures were being held hostage. We had to find a way to get them back.

Jeremiah said how the Graves would try to manipulate him to think that his family and friends didn't love him.

The same poison was poured down all our throats constantly when we lived with them; it was like there was no way to suck out the venom. It burned and at times was hard to breathe.

It was in too deep for too long but somehow, we broke free and found the antidote, our friends.

They saved us.

My brothers and I did go back to try and get my diary, our parents' pictures and other things that we weren't able to take with us before but they wouldn't let us in. We listened to our friends who told us that the best thing we could do is sue them and try to get back what we had lost.

The Graves never apologized.

Not for what they did. Not for the pain they caused. Instead, they turned to social media, twisting the story to make themselves look like the victims. They wanted sympathy. They wanted people to believe they were the ones who had been wronged, using my diary as a weapon against me when my family and I made the decision to sue them for what they did.

Adder thought of himself as perfect. He was raised to think that no matter what he did to others, he was always righteous. His disdain for people less fortunate was clear as he talked about them like they were trash that needed to be discarded. Perhaps that's how he felt about me and my family. Maybe that's why he would hurt me the way he did, he couldn't stand to look at me. He drank his privilege like it was fine wine. He loves to portray himself as a good Christian but that's a mask he wears to hide the evil festering within.

Our lawyers told me that his family was trying to enter my diary as evidence against my family but I was confused because I knew for sure that I didn't write anything bad in my diary.

Suddenly, I remembered Adder said that he had the perfect handwriting skills and could easily replicate other people's handwriting. I knew then what he had done.

He took my diary; copying my handwriting and making it appear as if I said things I never did. The only things I ever wrote in that diary was how much I missed my parents, how I felt about my classes, my friends and how much I hated it at that house with him and his family. I could imagine him enjoying ripping out the pages I had written and writing terrible things just to spite me but also, I knew his parents had a hand in it too.

The fact that they were trying to use one of the last things my father gifted to me was disgusting and just goes to show what kind of people they truly are.

I refused to let their lies define me. I knew the truth. God could see what they were doing and wasn't going to allow them to keep hurting my family.

Eventually, my brothers and I found refuge in the people who truly loved us — our real friends. People like Gloria, Andy, Sharon, Michelle, Crystal, Vicki, the Hayes' and so many others have helped my family through such a difficult time. We stayed with Gloria and her family for a time and they helped my oldest brother, Charles get his own apartment.

I ended up living with him, his girlfriend Christine and our brother Josh.

Slowly, life started to feel safe again.

But some wounds still ran deep.

My Other half

The Amezcuas were among those who
knew my family for years and treated us
like we were a part of theirs. My parents
met Nancy and Bobby Amezcua at one of
my middle school track meets. Their
daughters Cynthia and Debra were already
good friends with my older brothers
Charles, Michael and Jonathan. And then
there was Denise a.k.a. Shorty. She was very
energetic, full of life and always so happy. I
was too quiet and shy to think that she
would ever want to be friends with
someone like me. But that wasn't Denise;
she wanted me everywhere she was. Even
spending the night at her place, always
asking my parents for permission, which
they always agreed because, well she had
become so close to me that we were
inseparable, my other half. If we didn't

spend time together, it was as if we weren't complete. That's how much we loved each other. From trips to our favorite burger place, to having her mom make me an espresso for the first time, it was truly a blessing being with Denise and her family.

Sundays after church, my dad would always BBQ in this small grill outside. The aroma filled our two bedroom apartment and I couldn't wait to taste what my dad had made. Denise and her sisters sometimes came over along with some of our other friends like Mallisa and Eric. Mallisa got my attention by always staring at me at track practice. She said she would continue to do it until I started a conversation with her. She was always so silly. I loved her personality. Eric was Jeremiah and Josh's friend. They always hung out. Josh also had a best friend named Beau, blonde curly hair and just as tall as he was. They were like brothers. It didn't matter that we didn't have much and our place was small, our friends still wanted to be with us. My mom would be chatting on the phone with my Godmother Sharon about how much she enjoyed service that day and when their next girls hangout day would be. My mom loved this church in Downey. It was big and they were always so welcoming. She carried her bible with her, always excited for what the pastor had to say.

When we attended the Grave's church, my mom said after the service that it didn't feel right. I didn't know what she meant at the time but after living with the Graves and having to go there every Sunday with them, I understood exactly what she meant. The atmosphere was dull and heavy, a slight pressure on the chest. I never felt comfortable going there.

Denise and her family came over one night after my mother passed away. She walked up to my dad who was sitting inside on the edge of the bed, "Hi, Mr. Higgins, can we all take a picture together?" My dad, even though still hurting smiled and replied, "Yeah that's fine." The last photo of my dad alive was taken because of Denise.

The Promise

My brother Michael was a force on the football field. In high school he wore number 44 and in college, number 50. He played defense, but I remember him running the ball and scoring touchdowns too. Watching him play was always exciting — he truly loved the game. Our parents loved watching him play when he was at Downey High School, and I'll never forget the pride in their eyes every time he stepped onto the field.

There was even a time when Michael was mentioned on a high school sports segment on the news. Hearing his name on TV and listening to the reporters talk about how good of a player he was — that was an incredible moment. His team knew how powerful he was, and I remember hearing how some players on the other teams were afraid of getting tackled by him. At 6'0", built like he was made for football, Michael dominated the game with both skill and strength.

Every time I cheered for him from the stands, I couldn't help but think about how proud our mom and dad would be. And they were. Watching him play was one of their greatest joys.

My mom had once promised she'd be there when my team broke the school record for the Downey High School 4x400-meter relay that was set back in 1991. It stood at a time of 4:08.7, that's the time we needed to beat. I worked harder than ever, pushing myself with every step, hoping — praying — that she could still see me, looking down from Heaven. I trained with the distance coach to build up my endurance. Training with him was much harder than regular practice. He had me run the 800 meters at nearly every track meet leading up to my final race. It was difficult at first but soon I began to get good at it. If I remember correctly, my fastest time in the 800 meters was 2:18:00. It wasn't at an official league track meet, so I don't think that time was put into record. I'm grateful for Coach John for pushing me to be better in not just the 800 meters but the 400 meters as well.

Stephanie, Liz and Desiree were my 4x400 meter relay team. We trained hard since freshman year 2002. It was now 2006; two years after my parents had passed away.

The track was remodeled to be all-weather. I loved the bounce it gave but if you fell while running at full speed, it burned like hell. Still, we continued to train with our coach Amy. She was tough but also a lovely woman with the most beautiful soul. When she found out about my mother's cancer spreading, she told me not to worry about practice. I could see the pain in her eyes as she too loved my mom as many others did.

After my mother was gone, I told myself that I couldn't stop training. Even though it hurt, I had to keep going for her. I promised. I made a promise that I intended to keep. My team encouraged me and if I felt like I needed a breather to cry, they were there. I loved them. The entire track and field team showed up for my mother's funeral. The coaches, the boys team, the girls team, they were all there for my family, for my mom.

And of course, so many others were there as well.

And now, the day had finally arrived.

The CIF Prelims.

I had to do this, for my mom and for me.
My 4x400 relay team were like sisters to me.
Stephanie always seemed to be glowing.
She was radiantly charismatic, yet
effortlessly humble. She had a natural
beauty that turned heads, but her warmth
and kindness made her truly unforgettable.
Though she was outgoing and popular, she
never let status define her relationships. She

treated everyone with the same genuine care, making even the quietest person like myself, feel seen and valued. Stephanie's charm isn't just in her looks or popularity- it's in her ability to uplift others, bringing people together without judgment or pretense.

Liz was a firecracker wrapped in warmth- bold, outspoken, and unafraid to stand up for what's right, yet with endearing softness that made her easy to love. She had the spirit of a big sister, always looking out for others. Her black hair shimmered under the stadium lights, and her dazzling smile could lift anyone's spirits. Originally a 200- meter hurdler, Liz took on the challenge of the 400 meters and, eventually, the 4x400 relay, proving that her strength wasn't just in her speed, but in her heart and determination.

Lastly, Desiree had the grace of a model with a golden heart. Her long legs made her a natural on the track, but it was her sweet, lovable personality that made people gravitate toward her. She had a playful, silly side that could make anyone laugh, yet when the moment called for it, she was serious and reliable. Always there to listen, she had a way of comforting others with just her presence. Her beautiful hair was usually pulled back in a ponytail, but when she let it down, her curls danced in the wind, as effortlessly as she ran. With her combination of athleticism, kindness, and unwavering support, Desiree was the kind of friend who made every moment brighter.

My coach Amy was always encouraging us to keep pushing forward. Before the race she said, "Forget what I said, I want you to sprint the whole way! You will beat that record! Push it! Do it! Run!" I looked at my teammates. We were all still sad about my mom but wanted to do what we could to keep that promise.

This race meant a lot to us.

Our coach gave us a big thumbs up, smiled and embraced us. Her blonde hair fell to the side as it brushed my shoulder.

Before the race began, we prayed. Asking God to help us stay focused on not just the finish line but the time. As we stood up, we saw the other teams confidently getting in their lanes.

We hugged again and Liz said, "We've got this ladies!"

She waited in the blocks to hear the pop of the gun going off, hands behind the line. Ready.

There was a pause as we waited on the side lines nervously.

"BOOM!" The race began; it was Liz who led the charge. She quickly passed the other teams, there was a flame emitting from her cleats. Liz was flying! She came around the corner in ablaze. Desiree was next, second leg. Her long legs seemed to make her look so effortless when she ran, so graceful. Arms sketched out, here comes the baton. Stephanie was next, third leg. As soon as she got the baton, she bolted passed the competition. Our coach on the side lines cheering and giving me words of encouragement, "You're the last leg! Take us home!" I nodded, bouncing side to side ready to receive the baton. There she comes! Stephanie yelled, "Go!" She handed me the baton and I was off. Not paying attention to the other teams. I only focused on my speed, "Sprint the whole way!" The words echoing in my head. I make the last turn and can hear my mother's voice. I push with everything I've got. My legs felt like they were on fire. Burning! Burning! But I kept going until I crossed that finish line. I collapsed, crying, not wanting to hear that we didn't do it. My coach walked over to me and my sisters and said, "You did it! 4:07.28!" I couldn't believe it. We all hugged each other. Victory, for everything it meant.

And our 4x400 (1600M relay) record Stood
Strong for years after this day.

DOWNEY GIRLS TRACK & FIELD RECORDS			
100 M			
200 M	12.3	JASMINE BALDWIN	01
400 M	25.9	SHERONICA BAKER	96
800 M	59.8	LYNEE LOPEZ	98
600 M	2:22.9	PENNY MILLER	81
3200 M	5:18.4	PENNY MILLER	81
3 MILE	:26.64	MAGGIE CORTEZ	01
100 INT. HURDLES	18:39	KATRINA KWIECIEN	81
300 LOW HURDLES	15.1	ANT RES VICE	96
400 RELAY	46.76	ELIZABETH PEREYRA	07
1600M RELAY	49.4	BALDWIN, RAPADAS, CYRS MC KINLEY	01
	4:07.28	E. PEREYRA, D. SCOTT, C. HIGGINS S BRUTON	06
HIGH JUMP	5' 8'	KELLY BLACK	
LONG JUMP	17'6"	JA MINE BALD IN	84
TRIPLE JUMP	37'5"	ANT RES VICE	01
SHOT PUT	37'9"	ASHANTE BOOKER	97
DI CUS	115'7"	ZANEKA MB	94
POLE VAULT	11'6"	JO RAPADAS	97

All my brothers were there and cheered
looking proud. I looked around wanting to
see my mom but I knew she wouldn't be
there. I wanted to hug her too. To let her

know that I kept my promise and I wanted to celebrate with her.

Her brother Kevin was there though. He stood in the stands, cheering for me as if trying to carry her love in her absence.

And now, as I stood here in my prom dress, I wished — just like I had on that track — that she was still with me.

A Princess for a Night

The weight of the past few years clung to me, even as I stood in front of the mirror in my blue dress. My godmother's hands were gentle as she smoothed out the fabric, and then fussed with my hair, letting it fall naturally down my back. Just the way I wanted.

"You look beautiful, sweetheart," she said softly, but I struggled to believe it.

I had spent so long feeling invisible, unwanted and being told daily how ugly I was by the Graves.

I had asked people to go with me to prom. All of them said no.

"I'm not pretty enough" I thought,

"They didn't want to be seen with me."

Even after everything I had been through, their words still cut deep.

"It's true. I'm not pretty enough. I'm ugly." I kept thinking. The insults ringing in my ears, it was all I could think of.

When I got back from school that day, I laid in bed thinking what I should do. I rolled over on my side and was about to just give up when I had an idea.

My friend Amber lived just downstairs. She had a brother — Chris. We had all grown up together, and I had always thought he was so nice, always kind to everyone he met.

I was too nervous to ask him myself, so I asked Amber if she could do it for me.

She was so excited.

"I'll ask him right now!" she said, practically bouncing as she ran downstairs.

I waited.

My heart pounding.

Then, she returned, grinning.

"He wants to talk to you."

My stomach twisted into nervous knots as I made my way downstairs. The door opened, and there he was. Braces, shy smile—Chris.

"Hey," he said with a warm voice.

His mom was nearby, her face full of joy.
Then he said the words I never expected.

"Yeah, I'll go with you to prom."

I froze. I had prepared myself for rejection,
convinced I wasn't enough. But he said yes.

I barely managed to whisper a "thank you."

Before I had asked him to prom, I would see
him sometimes on my way home from
school. Chris was friends with my brothers
Jeremiah and Josh. They would hangout
sometimes after school. But, when I saw
him this time, he was by himself. His red
shirt had cut out sleeves and he wore black
shorts with white lines going down the
sides. Dark spiky hair and lightly tanned
skin stood out in the sunlight. He turned
and looked my way. I could see him waving

from the side of my eye but I kept walking. I was so shy back then and would act like I didn't see him. I power walked as fast as I could back home.

Prom dresses were pricey and I didn't want to spend a lot of money on one. I wanted to look nice but couldn't afford a fancy dress. I decided to buy fabric from a store my mom and I would always go to. We loved Joanns. It was a big store that had a wide variety of fabrics to choose from. They had very pretty colors and I knew exactly the color I wanted to wear, cerulean blue.

I filled my basket with all I needed and headed for the checkout. The woman who helped me had a big smile on her face as she knew I was gathering supplies for prom. After I checked out she said, "I hope you have fun!" I smiled and thanked her, trying to hide the huge grin on my face.

Shopping for my shoes was tricky because I didn't usually wear heels and was nervous. I found some pretty ones in the mall. When I tried them on, they felt like they would be comfortable. My friend Marie looked at my choice of shoes with slight concern, "Are you sure you want those? Did you try walking in them?"

"Yes. They felt fine to me. These are pretty. The silver will match my dress." I replied thinking I had found the perfect pair of shoes.

I met Marie my freshman year of high school. It was the first day of school and the teacher wanted the class to get to know each other. So, we all shared something interesting about ourselves and our favorite hobbies. When the teacher called my name, I hesitated to stand up because I wasn't comfortable speaking to a lot of people. I took a while to say anything but finally said, "I like to draw and I like running." I then quickly sat back down. Marie stared at me unsure if she should say anything but when the teacher wasn't looking, she poked me and said, "You draw? I like drawing too." I was a bit startled but nodded and smiled.

Marie had shoulder length hair that was reddish brown with light highlights.

After class, she followed me and began asking so many questions about what I liked to draw and if I wanted to hang out sometime. It was a lot all at once but I stopped walking, turned to her and said, "Okay but I'll have to ask my mom"

I asked my mom that night and the next day, Marie and her mom, Gloria came by to meet my parents. My Godmother Sharon was also there and they all chatted and laughed about a variety of topics. I was happy. My mom exchanged phone numbers with Gloria and they set up a date for Marie and me to hang out at her house.

Marie is very soft spoken like myself. We are alike in a lot of ways and I think that's another reason why we became close.

I had decided on the shoes despite Marie's protests. We looked around the mall for a bit longer before Marie's mom came to pick us up and drop me back home.

I made spaghetti for everyone that night as Charles and Josh played video games and Christine made the salad, "I love this." I thought. Seeing my brothers happy made me smile. The lawsuit was still on going, but for now, I wanted to forget about that family and focus on my own happiness.

After dinner, I went to my room and stared at myself in my bathroom mirror. I didn't feel pretty enough. I thought, "I'm going to look stupid in that dress, Chris is going to be embarrassed to be seen with me" Bad thoughts kept rolling around in my head.

Christine's grandmother had offered to make my prom dress. I was nervous about how it would turn out but I was also confident in their abilities and trusted that they would do a good job making my dress.

The night of prom arrived, I was shaking. Gloria suggested we all met at her house to take pictures. She had a beautiful garden in the backyard. It was so pretty with the flowers and small pond; I anxiously waited for Chris to arrive, my brothers playfully teased me. I paced back and forth but then finally, he was there. My eyes lit up and I couldn't stop smiling, he looked so handsome. He walked over to me as I stood in the middle of the parterre. His smile was quiet but full of meaning-shy, almost hesitant curve of his lips, like he wasn't sure if he should smile but couldn't help it. There was softness to it, warmth that made it feel special, like it was meant just for me. His eyes held a quiet understanding, and in that moment, his smile said everything he didn't need to put into words.

For the first time in a long time, I felt truly happy.

It was fun having us all there together. My cerulean blue dress shimmered in the evening light, and Chris — his tie perfectly matching me — stood beside me. I couldn't stop smiling. Pictures! Pictures and more pictures! So much fun but my face was starting to hurt from smiling so much.

Later we headed to Denise's place and took pictures by a sleek blue motorcycle. Chris sat on it effortlessly, looking so cool, so natural, like he had always belonged there.

Then the classic cars arrived, polished, vintage, and elegant. They looked like something out of an old Hollywood movie. Red, blue and black, Denise shined next to the red one, as her dress matched it so perfectly. She motioned Chris and me to get into the blue one. We hurried as we slid inside, Chris pulled me close.

The driver had the window down the whole way there, my hair was flying everywhere. Chris kept brushing it back down. I felt so embarrassed thinking maybe I should have put my hair up but he just smiled at me.

When we arrived at the Aquarium in Long Beach, my breath caught.

The water, the glow of the lights, the massive glass tanks — it was magical.

I spotted my track coach and rushed to hug her. She was wearing a pretty yellow dress.

"I'm so happy you're here!" she said, her voice full of pride. Then she turned to Chris, sizing him up before nodding in approval.

We found our table, but the music soon started playing. Denise and her date tried to get us to dance but it was upbeat music and I didn't feel like dancing at the moment.

I turned to my date and said, "Can we go upstairs?" I whispered to Chris.

He didn't hesitate. He took my hand and led me up the winding stairs.

The upper level was nearly empty, bathed in the soft blue glow of the water. Fish swam lazily behind the glass, their movements' hypnotic.

"Would you like to sit down?" He asked. I nodded; my heels weren't very kind to my feet. I didn't wear heels often and wasn't used to them. I had on very low heels but they were still killing my feet. I sat down as he stood up looking over at the fish in the large tanks, then he turned his gaze at me and smiled.

"Sorry, I didn't realize these heels would hurt like this." I said embarrassed. He chuckled and said, "Don't worry. I didn't really want to dance right now anyway."

My expression soon changed.

"What's wrong?" He asked.

Little did he know it would take me nearly the whole night to confess what was on my mind but he was so patient and only cared about making sure I was okay. Never did he appear annoyed, only showing concern. He probably thought I was feeling tired because of how hard it was to stand in my heels. It wasn't my feet though. I was unsure if I should tell him what was on my mind. Not sure how he would respond but this was my one chance and after high school, we probably wouldn't get the chance to be alone like this again.

Finally, I couldn't hold it in anymore.

I mustered everything within me to say,

"I… I like you." My voice was barely above a whisper.

He looked at me, his expression unreadable.

Finally, he said,

"I can't give you an answer. Not right now." he admitted his voice kind and calm. "But I want you to have the best night. This is your night."

Then, as if the universe had heard him, the music changed, a slow song. It was time for the final dance of the night.

Chris didn't hesitate, we rushed downstairs. He took my hand, pulled me close, and we danced. For some reason, my feet didn't hurt anymore. I rested my head against his chest, feeling the steady rhythm of his heartbeat. I felt so happy, safe in his arms.

He pulled back just enough to look at me, his voice soft, "You're beautiful."

I nearly broke down.

For years, I had been told I wasn't pretty. But here, in his arms, I felt like a princess, dancing with the most handsome boy I had ever laid eyes on, a real life prince.

The song seemed to play on forever, and we danced as if nothing else in the world mattered.

I closed my eyes and felt like I was in a dream. All the pain had disappeared and I felt like I was floating. It felt like clouds under my feet lifting me high. Chris was holding me closer. He was careful not to step on my feet. I could tell he had practiced a lot just to make this night special for me. His movements were like those of a professional dancer. I didn't want to let go but the song ended. His hands still firmly holding onto me, one hand on my waist and the other holding my right hand. I knew eventually he would have to let go and I didn't want him to.

But he did.

We walked over to our group that was waiting for us and together we headed outside to wait for our limbo.

On the limo ride home, exhaustion crept in.

"Lay down," Chris murmured, patting his lap.

I rested my head against him, letting my eyes drift closed.

When I awoke, we had arrived home. He helped me to the front door of my apartment and we said goodbye as he went down stairs.

I'm not sure if it was the day after or a week or two but eventually Chris and I talked again. We cared about each other, but the both of us were still growing, still figuring out who we were meant to be. Chris understood that after everything I had been through, I needed space to truly find myself. So, he gently said, "I'm sorry, Charis." I replied, "It's okay. Thank you."

I remember curling up in bed that night, crying into my pillow. It hurt, he was the first boy I had ever loved but he was right. I was still dealing with my past and he needed to decide what he wanted in life and I respected that.

I never told him everything that happened in that house. He knew some things but I was too ashamed to tell him anything else. I didn't want him to be sad. I wanted him to be happy. He deserved so much happiness.

We have remained close friends, choosing to support each other from a distance. He seems so far away but I'm very proud of everything he has been able to accomplish in life. He has really found himself and I'm so happy. We went our separate ways, but not really-because even now, through all of life's twists and turns, Chris still checks in.

We have an unspoken bond that time and distance couldn't break, true friendship.

He was the light that I needed to bring me back to life and now; he remains one of my dearest friends. All I want to say to him is:

Dear Chris,

Thank you for saving me that day. Because of you, I gained confidence in myself and felt worthy of being loved. Thank you for being a gentleman. For making me feel like everything would be okay. Thank you for being nice to me, for making my prom so very special. It was like a fairy-tale and I felt like a princess. Thank you for just being you. I wish you so much happiness and love. You will forever be special to me and I will cherish you always.

-With Love,

Charis ♡

Art School and a Brother's Love

After graduating high school, I received a scholarship to attend an art school. It was an exciting opportunity, but the school was far from home. To get there, I had to take three trains and two buses, which made for a long commute. I didn't have a car, and my family was always busy working, so I figured out the route on my own. I wanted to be independent.

My brother Charles, always the protective older brother, made sure I had enough money for transportation and meals. "If you're ever short, just let me know," he'd say, pressing a few extra bills into my hand before I left. His quiet support meant a lot to me.

Art school itself was… different. My first class was with a teacher who barely spoke.

He handed out the assignment with little explanation, saying only, "Draw this." It was a ball. We had to shade it realistically, capturing the light and shadows perfectly. It wasn't difficult, but the class could be painfully dull.

English class was more engaging. One day, we were assigned to write about someone who inspired us. I thought of many people, but in the end, I wrote about my parents. That assignment made me reflect on ways I could honor their memory. That's when I started writing a story at home — a story that would later become my manga series, Kisara's Moon.

Despite being grateful for the scholarship, I couldn't shake the feeling that art school wasn't for me. Every day, I kept thinking, I don't need art school to be an artist. The realization became unavoidable when the school called me in to discuss tuition for the next semester. My scholarship only covered the first semester, and the next one would cost over $2,500. I couldn't afford it. Sitting in that office, looking at the numbers, I knew there was no way I could continue.

Dropping out wasn't an easy decision. I wanted to keep learning, but I also knew that some things I could teach myself. So, I left art school and focused on improving my art on my own. I spent my free time writing, drawing, and trying to enjoy life. I didn't want to think about the Graves.

One afternoon, I was leaving the mall when I unexpectedly ran into my brother Jonathan.

"Let's go back inside," he said, motioning for me to step back through the double doors.

"Um... why?" I asked, confused. I had already finished browsing, but maybe he wanted to hang out.

"Those shoes suck. I'm buying you new ones," he said, eyes locked on a shoe store ahead.

I looked down at my shoes. They were a little worn, but I didn't think much of it. I was used to making things last. But Jonathan, being my big brother, just wanted to make sure I was taking care of myself.

"You know, Charles said he was going to buy me new shoes but I said 'no' because I figured these had at least another month or two in them." I said with a grin. "I think just black shoes. See, those are cheap. I could get those."

Jonathan gave me a look but let me pick. I wasn't the type to go for fancy things. We didn't grow up with much, so I learned early on to appreciate what we had. But I was grateful he wanted to do this for me.

"Why do you always wear black?" he asked as I tried on a pair.

"It matches my mood most days," I joked. "Kidding. I don't know. I just like wearing black, I guess."

Jonathan just shook his head and grabbed the box, taking it straight to the cashier before I could argue.

We walked around the mall a bit longer, and then he said he had to meet up with some friends. I waved goodbye, telling him to be safe. That was Jonathan — outgoing, friendly, always surrounded by people. But no matter what, we always made time for each other. He would call me every week, and we'd talk about the most random things. He always made me laugh.

He passed away in 2023.

His death still weighs so heavily on me. We were so close, and I don't understand why he's not here anymore. I still want to call him, ask him the things I never got to. But I can't.

He's gone.

And I'm still struggling to accept that.

Gonzo

In 2007, I started working at a small movie theater in Downey. The job was fun, but I hated the uniform — white dress shirt, black dress pants, an oversized red belt, and a black bow tie. The worst part was the white shirt. I worked in concessions most of the time, and no matter how careful I was, butter stains were unavoidable. Those shirts were nearly impossible to clean, and replacements cost around $20 each. Who in their right mind thought white was a good choice for people handling popcorn and nacho cheese?

Despite the uniform, I enjoyed the job. Customers could be a hit or miss, though. Some were friendly, others were rude — especially if they were late to their movie and needed someone to blame. One of my least favorite tasks was working the podium, where we weren't allowed to let anyone in with outside food. I always followed the rules, but I felt bad. Movie theater snacks were expensive, and I knew not everyone could afford them. My go-to order was simple — a lightly salted pretzel and a slushy.

One afternoon, I was running late for my shift, practically speed-walking to clock in on time. That's when I bumped into a guy with thick glasses and spiky hair.

"Hey, you want one? I bet you do. Five bucks each. You look like a size small," he said grinning as he held up a T-shirt.

"Huh? No, I have to clock in," I said, rushing past him.

I barely made it — punching in my code and pressing my hand on the scanner just in time. Ding! I was safe.

Concessions again.

As I walked through the back door to the front counter, I saw the same spiky-haired guy standing at the register.

"You work here?" I asked, confused.

"And so do you. Crazy, right?" he teased.

What a smart-ass.

I rolled my eyes and went on with my shift. It wasn't a particularly busy day, so it passed quickly. As I was getting ready to leave, I felt a tap on my shoulder.

"Hey, Miss, did you want a shirt?"

"Oh, I don't have change right now. Maybe next time I see you at work," I said, not even sure what his shirts looked like.

He pulled one from his backpack and handed it to me. "Here you go. You get one free. Next one, you have to pay."

I smiled as I unfolded the black T-shirt. The design on it was a white octopus—bold and intricate. It was cool.

"Gonzo," he said suddenly, completely straight-faced.

"What?" I blinked, unsure if I missed something.

"That's its name. The octopus. It's called Gonzo. I designed it. You like it?"

"I do. It's really cool," I said. Then I realized I hadn't introduced myself. "Oh, I never told you my name. It's—"

"Yes, Miss, it's Charis. I know. I'm Joseph. Nice to meetcha. Again, haha."

Joseph was... different. Funny, sarcastic, and a little weird, but in a good way. We became friends instantly and started hanging out outside of work.

One time, he was driving me somewhere and took a shortcut through an alleyway. Out of nowhere, something darted past us.

"Raccoon!" I shouted.

Joseph burst into laughter. "That wasn't a raccoon! That was an opossum!"

We argued about it the whole way.

Joseph was also in a band called Papersails. Their music was unique — indie surf, definitely not what you heard on the radio. I went to several of their shows, and it was always a good time.

He became one of my closest friends — someone who never judged me and was always there to listen.

Even now, I'm grateful for that.

Among the Twinkling Stars

The months passed, and I kept wondering when this lawsuit with the Graves would finally end. I knew it was a long process, but the waiting filled me with anxiety. I wanted justice for my family, but deep down, I feared the Graves would somehow manipulate the system again, just as they always had.

It was April 2007, and I was home alone, sitting at my computer. Everyone else had gone out, but I wasn't in the mood to go anywhere. There was this dating site people had been using, and out of boredom, I decided to check it out. I wasn't looking for anything serious — I just wanted to see if anyone would actually message me back.

I must have sent a dozen random "Hello!" or "What's up?" messages, not expecting any replies. Then, out of nowhere, a message popped up.

"Hey."

I stared at the screen for a while, debating whether to respond. It took me maybe an hour before I finally typed back.

"How are you?"

They responded, "Good. What are you doing?"

I replied sarcastically, "Talking to you."

That made him laugh. His username gave me a clue about his name, so I asked what it was. He replied:

"Eddie. And yours?"

"Charis." I replied.

"That's Greek, right? It means grace." Eddie said confidently.

I smiled to myself, convinced he had just looked that up to impress me.

"That's right. Congrats!" I was starting to enjoy talking to him.

I found out later that he knew my brother Jonathan since middle school. He said he was really quiet back then; Jonathan noticed and gave him one of his pens to start up a conversation. Eddie said that Jonathan was the first person that he could really call his friend at the time. They remained very good friends up to the very end.

We kept talking that night, and before I knew it, we had spent hours chatting. Every day after that, we talked more and more. I started looking forward to his messages. Eventually, we decided to meet in person, with Christine's younger sister, Bebe, tagging along as my chaperone.

We met at a coffee shop. He had super curly, fluffy hair and wore a white top with blue jeans. His pale skin had a mole on his left cheek, and he wore glasses that suited him well. He bought me a coffee while Bebe kept a close watch, making sure he was respectful. We only hung out for about thirty minutes before we had to leave, but I found myself thinking he was cute.

A few weeks later, after a movie night, Eddie asked me to be his girlfriend. I hesitated. I had never been in a relationship before, and I wasn't sure what I wanted. I told Bebe about my uncertainty, and she gave me the best advice:

"If you're not 100% sure, then say no. Do what feels right for you."

I thought long and hard. My mind kept running through all the possible scenarios.

What if I said no?

Well, I'd stay single forever, I guess.

What if I said yes?

Then I'd have a boyfriend. That would be... interesting.

A few days later, I finally gave him my answer.

"Yes."

And in time, I grew to truly care about him. About a year later, we got married. Crazy, I know. But it felt right. We had so much in common, and I believed he was a good person.

Not long after we got married, everything with the lawsuit seemed to speed into overdrive.

I still remember the day I walked into that office and saw Adder sitting there with his mother. My body nearly froze. Memories flooded my mind — memories of being pinned down, insulted, mocked.

"You're weak. Fight back!"

"Ugly!"

"Mute!"

I just wanted it to be over. I wanted to never see them again.

And finally, that day came.

My brothers and I met with our lawyers, who assured us that the Graves wouldn't be able to use my diary against us. The ruling came down: the Graves were ordered to pay for what they had done and for the money they had stolen from us. I felt a wave of relief wash over me.

But, of course, they refused.

They were supposed to make monthly payments, but they ignored the order completely. For a while, it seemed like they would get away with it yet again. Then, we received news that changed everything — somehow, the Graves had been forced to pay the full amount all at once.

They had finally faced real consequences for their actions.

And yet, even in the face of undeniable truth, they refused to admit any wrongdoing. They called my family liars, pretending they had never paid us a dime. They lived in a constant state of delusion.

But that's how narcissists are. They gaslight, deflect, and twist reality, always trying to make themselves the victims. Even after everything, they created fake social media accounts, spreading lies about my family, even attacking my parents. It was sickening.

The Graves had always been evil — wolves in sheep's clothing, hiding behind Christianity as a shield. But they were never real Christians. They never cared about anything but themselves.

Through it all, I endured more than I ever thought I could. But I wasn't alone.

Along the way, I was surrounded by people who truly cared about me, the people who lifted me up when I felt like I couldn't stand. People who reminded me that I was worth more than the pain the Graves had inflicted.

To those people, I hope you know how much you mean to me.

I want my daughter to know that her mom never gave up. Even when the weight of my past tried to pull me down, I kept pushing forward. And I did it because of the people who saved me from sinking completely into the darkness.

Those people mean the world to me. If I could, I would do anything to repay their kindness.

As I look up at the night sky, I see the stars twinkling down at me — reminders of the love and guidance from those I've lost.

And I smile, knowing that they are proud of me.

I love you.

In Loving Memory

My Dad and Mom

My brother Jonathan

You are forever in our hearts and never forgotten....

I love you

A Message to my readers

It took me years to decide to write this book. I was afraid of what that family might say and I was ashamed thinking that in telling my story that I was somehow doing something wrong. The Graves made me feel like I had to stay silent and that how I was feeling didn't matter. I know now that's not true. It's never wrong to speak your mind and say exactly what you are feeling. In this book, I let out all my raw emotions. I am not ashamed to do that anymore because this is how I feel. Every word, I meant it. Even though it was hard, I'm glad I finally let go and said what I've wanted to say for so long now.

About the author

Charis Alfonso is an author, artist, and creator of the magical girl manga series *Kisara's Moon* and the fantasy romance novel *The Tale of Jakob and the Kitsune*. With a passion for storytelling that blends adventure, romance, and deep emotional themes, she crafts narratives that resonate with readers through compelling characters and heartfelt journeys.

From a young age, Charis found solace in writing, using it as a way to express emotions, navigate life's challenges, and bring to life the stories that lived in her heart. Her works often explore themes of love, friendship, perseverance, and the search for identity, drawing inspiration from personal experiences, cherished memories, and the people who have shaped her life.

When she's not writing, she enjoys creating art, animating, playing video games and working on new projects for her small business, where she sells stickers, key chains, bookmarks, and more. A lover of anime, magical girl stories, and nostalgic trips to the mall, she finds joy in the little things and strives to capture that same magic in her work.

She is also a devoted mother who encourages her daughter's creativity and love for dinosaurs, always reminding her to cherish the world around her. Through her writing, Charis hopes to inspire others to chase their dreams, hold onto hope, and find strength in their own stories.

Thank you for reading